SandCastle™

Primeros Sonidos

I0880494

Zenaida y Zenobio

Cathy Camarena, M.Ed., and Gloria B. Ruff, M.Ed.

Consulting Editors

Lourdes Flores-Hanson, M.S.E., and Gloria Rosso-White

ABDO Publishing Company

capstone®

www.capstoneclassroom.com

Credits
Curriculum Coordinator: Nancy Tuminelly
Cover and Interior Design and Production: Mighty Media
Child Photography: Steven Wewerka, Wewerka Photography
Photo Credits: AbleStock, Photodisc

ISBN 978-1-4966-0383-8 (paperback)

Printed in the United States of America in North Mankato, Minnesota.
012015 008756

SandCastle™ books are created by a professional team of educators, reading specialists, and content developers around five essential components that include phonemic awareness, phonics, vocabulary, text comprehension, and fluency. All books are written, reviewed, and leveled for guided and early intervention reading, and designed for use in shared, guided, and independent reading and writing activities to support a balanced approach to literacy instruction.

SandCastle Level: Beginning

Zz

ABCChDEFGH
IJKLLLMNÑOP
QRSTUVWXYZ

abcchdefgh
ijklllmnñop
qrstuvwxyz

Zenaida

Zenobio

zorro

zigzag

zapatos

zorrillo

zapatillas

Mira el  .

Mira el .

Mira los .

Mira el  .

Mira las  .

A Zenobio le gusta caminar en zigzag.

El zigzag es amarillo.

A Zenaida le gusta el zorrillo.

El zorrillo tiene pelo suave.

El zorrillo tiene una cola.

Al zorrillo también le gusta caminar en zigzag.

¿Cuáles de estas cosas comienzan con z?

Más palabras que comienzan con z

zacate

zanahoria

zancos

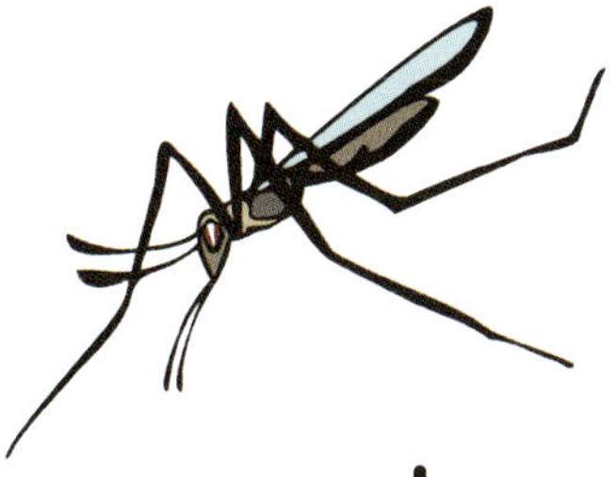

zancudo

zuecos

About SandCastle™

A professional team of educators, reading specialists, and content developers created the SandCastle™ series to support young readers as they develop reading skills and strategies and increase their general knowledge. The SandCastle™ series has four levels that correspond to early literacy development in young children. The levels are provided to help teachers and parents select the appropriate books for young readers.

Emerging Readers
(no flags)

Beginning Readers
(1 flag)

Transitional Readers
(2 flags)

Fluent Readers
(3 flags)

These levels are meant only as a guide. All levels are subject to change.

ABDO Publishing Company
www.abdopub.com

capstone
www.capstoneclassroom.com